Texas
Seashore Life

Includes:

Texas Ecoregions

Habitats and Habits

Bird Activities

Mammal Activities

Fish Activities

Reptile & Amphibian Activities

Invertebrate Activities

Plant Activities

T0009030

Waterford Press
www.waterfordpress.com

Introduction

The Texas seashore is a narrow band about 60 miles wide stretching 367 miles (591 km) along the Texas coast. Along this seashore are shallow bays, estuaries, salt marshes, dunes, tidal flats and Gulf waters that are all rich in wildlife. There are many important wildlife sanctuaries and refuges in the Gulf prairies and marshes that are safe places and home to thousands of animal species.

Ecoregions are areas that share the same climate, geology, soils, wildlife and land formations. There are 10 different ecoregions in Texas and the seashore is in the Gulf Prairies and Marshes region.

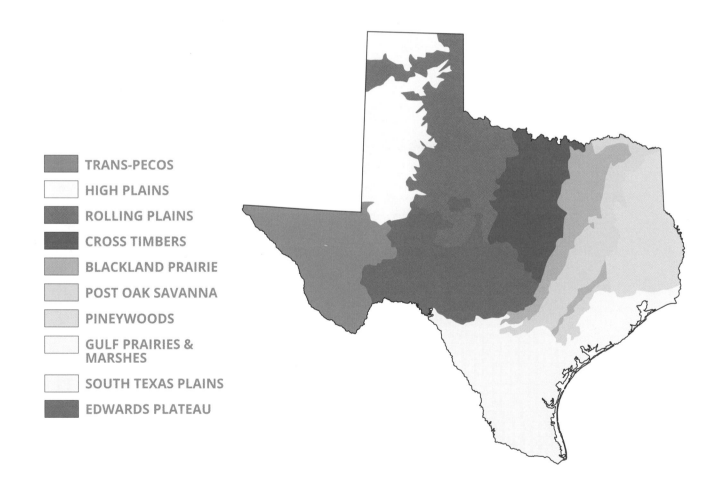

TRANS-PECOS

HIGH PLAINS

ROLLING PLAINS

CROSS TIMBERS

BLACKLAND PRAIRIE

POST OAK SAVANNA

PINEYWOODS

GULF PRAIRIES & MARSHES

SOUTH TEXAS PLAINS

EDWARDS PLATEAU

Texas Ecoregions

Trans-Pecos
From desert valleys and plains to wooded mountains, the Trans-Pecos region extends from the far west part of Texas to the Pecos River.

High Plains
The High Plains is a fairly level plateau. The Caprock Escarpment separates it from the Rolling Plains.

Rolling Plains
The Rolling Plains is where many rivers and tributaries in Texas begin.

Cross Timbers
The Cross Timbers area has a lot of trees as well as irregular prairies and plains. It is found in north and central Texas.

Blackland Prairie
This region gets its name from the fertile, black soils for which it is known.

Post Oak Savanna
There are many plants and animals here with ranges that extend as far east as the forests and as far north as the Great Plains.

Pineywoods
The Pineywoods in East Texas are home to forests of tall hardwoods and rolling hills covered with oaks and pines.

Gulf Prairies & Marshes
Streams and rivers divide this nearly level plain as they flow into the Gulf of Mexico.

South Texas Plains
This region is known for its subtropical woodlands and patches of palms, as well as thorny shrubs and trees.

Edwards Plateau
Known for spring-fed rivers and stony hills, Edwards Plateau is part of an area sometimes called Texas Hill Country.

Class Act

Animals can be sorted into categories based on certain characteristics. The system for sorting animals into categories is called taxonomy. Mammals, birds, fish, reptiles and amphibians belong to a class of animals called vertebrates. Vertebrates are animals with backbones. Invertebrates are another class of animals that do not have backbones (like insects, worms, snails, lobsters, crabs and spiders).

Draw a line between the animal and the class to which it belongs.

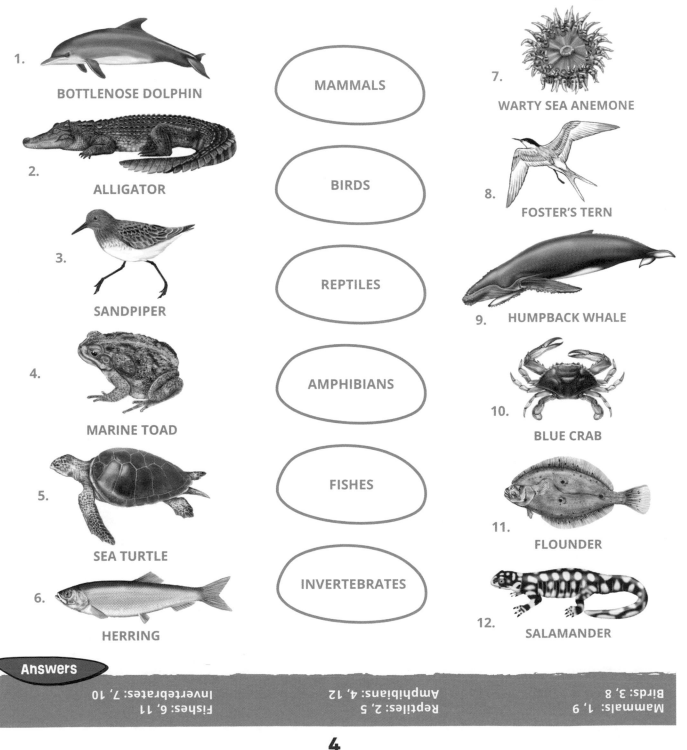

1. BOTTLENOSE DOLPHIN

2. ALLIGATOR

3. SANDPIPER

4. MARINE TOAD

5. SEA TURTLE

6. HERRING

MAMMALS

BIRDS

REPTILES

AMPHIBIANS

FISHES

INVERTEBRATES

7. WARTY SEA ANEMONE

8. FOSTER'S TERN

9. HUMPBACK WHALE

10. BLUE CRAB

11. FLOUNDER

12. SALAMANDER

You Are What You Eat

Herbivores eat mostly plants.
Carnivores eat mostly animals.
Omnivores eat plants and animals.

Draw a line between the seashore animal and its diet.

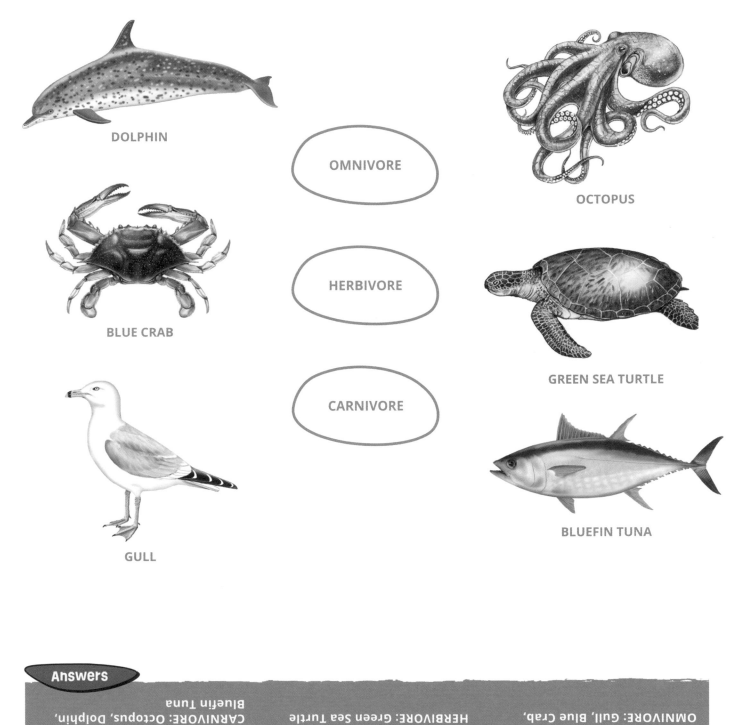

DOLPHIN

OMNIVORE

OCTOPUS

BLUE CRAB

HERBIVORE

GREEN SEA TURTLE

CARNIVORE

BLUEFIN TUNA

GULL

Food Chain

A food chain is the order in which animals feed on other plants and animals. All living things need each other. For instance, a simple food chain might be: crab to jellyfish to sea turtle.

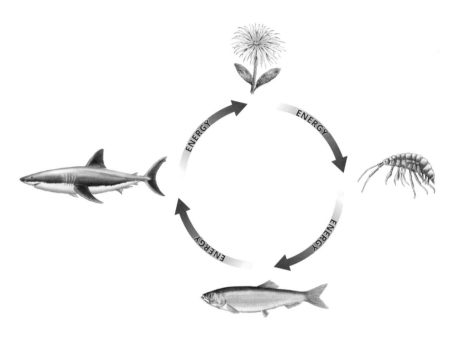

Producers – A producer takes the sun's energy and stores it as food.

Consumers – A consumer feeds on other living things to get energy. Consumers can include herbivores, carnivores and omnivores.

Decomposers – A decomposer consumes waste and dead organisms for energy.

Label each living organism below as a producer, consumer or decomposer.

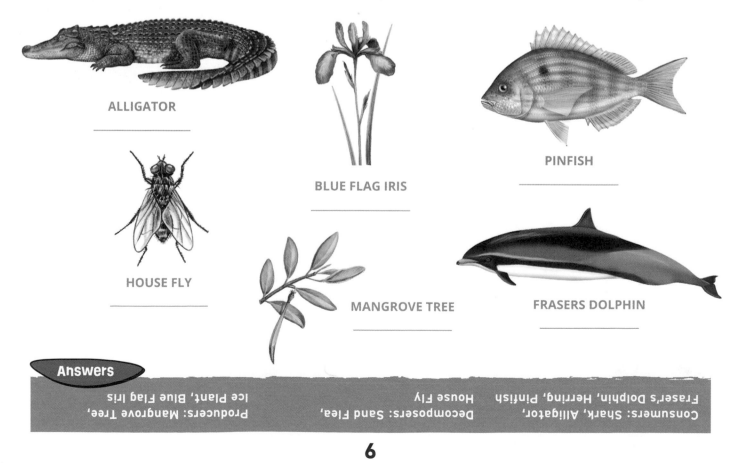

ALLIGATOR

_____

HOUSE FLY

_____

BLUE FLAG IRIS

_____

MANGROVE TREE

_____

PINFISH

_____

FRASERS DOLPHIN

_____

Find My Home

A habitat provides the things an animal needs for survival: food, shelter, water, the right temperature and protection from predators (animals who prey on other living things).

Draw a line between the animal and its habitat.

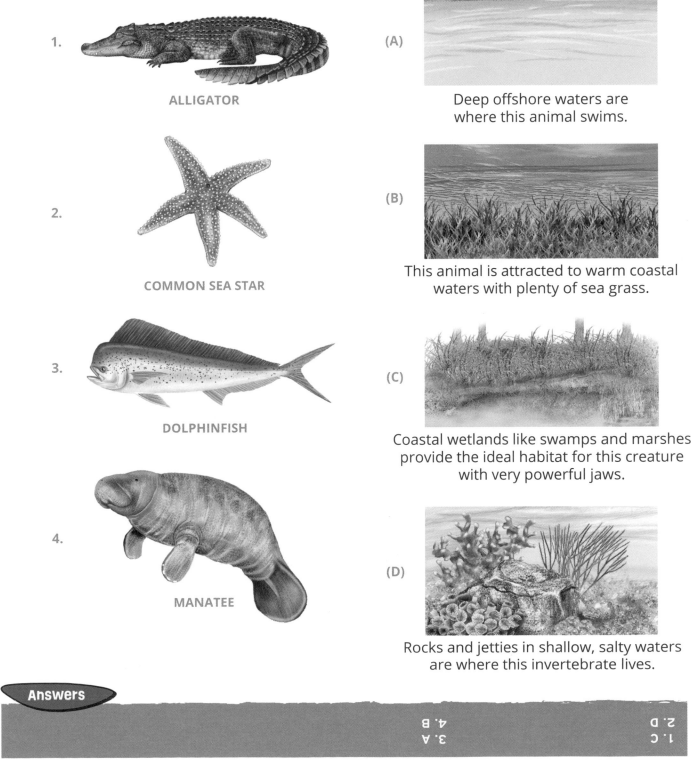

1. **ALLIGATOR**

2. **COMMON SEA STAR**

3. **DOLPHINFISH**

4. **MANATEE**

(A) Deep offshore waters are where this animal swims.

(B) This animal is attracted to warm coastal waters with plenty of sea grass.

(C) Coastal wetlands like swamps and marshes provide the ideal habitat for this creature with very powerful jaws.

(D) Rocks and jetties in shallow, salty waters are where this invertebrate lives.

Word Search

Coastal marshes are home to hundreds of thousands of wintering geese and ducks. Coastal dunes offer haven for north-bound Peregrine Falcons in the fall, and hundreds of other species live near Texas's coastal waters year-round.

Find the names of these nearshore birds in the puzzle.

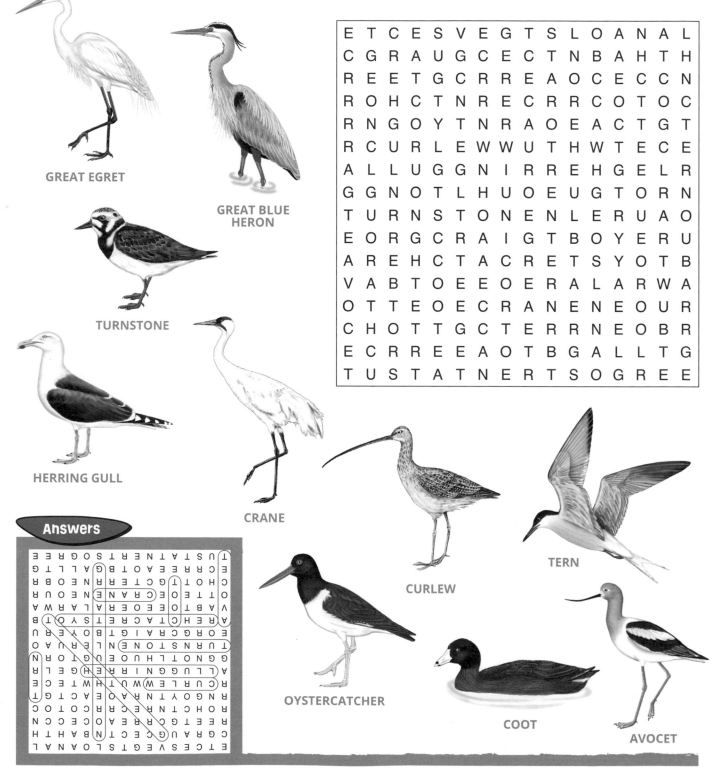

GREAT EGRET

GREAT BLUE HERON

TURNSTONE

HERRING GULL

CRANE

E	T	C	E	S	V	E	G	T	S	L	O	A	N	A	L
C	G	R	A	U	G	C	E	C	T	N	B	A	H	T	H
R	E	E	T	G	C	R	R	E	A	O	C	E	C	C	N
R	O	H	C	T	N	R	E	C	R	R	C	O	T	O	C
R	N	G	O	Y	T	N	R	A	O	E	A	C	T	G	T
R	C	U	R	L	E	W	W	U	T	H	W	T	E	C	E
A	L	L	U	G	G	N	I	R	R	E	H	G	E	L	R
G	G	N	O	T	L	H	U	O	E	U	G	T	O	R	N
T	U	R	N	S	T	O	N	E	N	L	E	R	U	A	O
E	O	R	G	C	R	A	I	G	T	B	O	Y	E	R	U
A	R	E	H	C	T	A	C	R	E	T	S	Y	O	T	B
V	A	B	T	O	E	E	O	E	R	A	L	A	R	W	A
O	T	T	E	O	E	C	R	A	N	E	N	E	O	U	R
C	H	O	T	T	G	C	T	E	R	R	N	E	O	B	R
E	C	R	R	E	E	A	O	T	B	G	A	L	L	T	G
T	U	S	T	A	T	N	E	R	T	S	O	G	R	E	E

Answers

TERN

CURLEW

OYSTERCATCHER

COOT

AVOCET

Oystercatchers are beautiful wading birds that are seen along shorelines searching for shellfish, crabs and other invertebrates.

Help this Oystercatcher find the oyster.

ENTER

Name Scramble

Unscramble the letters to form the names of these common seashore birds.

1.

LULG

2.

NPAEILC

3.

WRLEUC

4.

NOBOLSPIL

5.

NEORH

6.

SOGOE

7.

MOCROATNR

8.

KUDC

10

Crossword Puzzle

Animals living in salt marshes must be able to tolerate the saltiness and changes in water levels brought on by the tides and freshwater that flows in. Mammals are drawn to the abundant seeds and leaves of the marsh plants. Many mammals that live here are small, quick and elusive.

Use the clues about salt marsh mammals to help solve the puzzle.

Across

4. This is a semi-aquatic (living partly in or near water) North American rodent.
6. Though "river" is in its name, this animal also makes salt marshes its home.
8. This animal is tough to find because it likes to be alone and is active mostly at night.

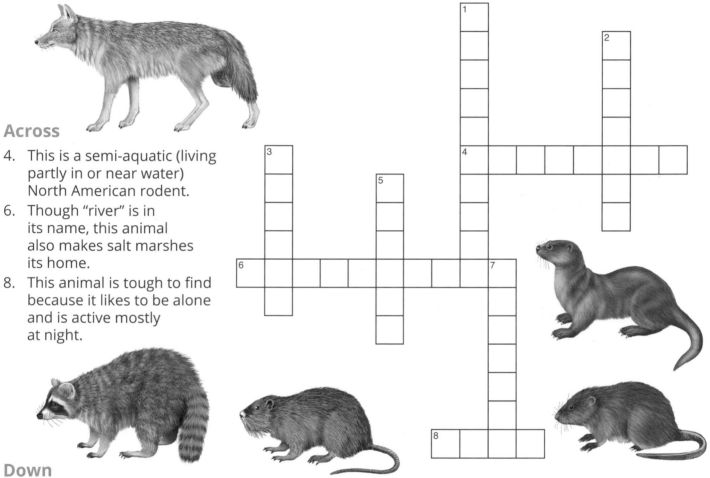

Down

1. This endangered species comes to the salt marsh to feed on the plant matter found there.
2. This animal has a long, scaly rudder-like tail that is flattened on both sides.
3. This invasive species was introduced to the United States because of its fur An invasive species is a living thing that was introduced to a new place where it didn't belong and can cause harm to the environment.
5. This dog-like mammal comes to the salt marsh to hunt the smaller animals that feed there.
7. This animal is an omnivore that visits the salt marsh during low tide to eat crabs, shrimp, fish or anything in its diet.

Word Search

Marine mammals are a group of mammals with unique body parts or behaviors that help them thrive in ocean habitats, where temperatures, depths, pressure and darkness are extreme. There are 28 species of marine mammals living in the waters of the Gulf of Mexico.

Find the names of these marine mammals.

MINKE WHALE

KILLER WHALE

PILOT WHALE

SPERM WHALE

K	P	R	P	K	W	W	B	E	L	E	A	F	E	E	P	O	P
I	D	O	I	T	E	T	A	A	A	L	A	I	N	N	E	L	B
L	A	N	L	L	I	T	W	L	M	A	E	N	E	I	I	G	S
L	K	I	O	A	L	H	W	P	I	W	Y	W	L	H	O	I	W
E	M	H	T	R	E	I	A	M	W	P	W	H	A	P	L	O	I
R	O	P	W	N	N	A	B	P	P	P	A	A	H	L	T	D	W
W	I	L	H	S	H	W	I	W	H	M	M	L	W	O	O	O	W
H	L	O	A	P	P	N	I	W	W	D	I	E	K	D	A	I	E
A	H	D	L	W	S	E	B	A	O	P	N	L	C	D	F	R	H
L	W	R	E	L	W	H	R	E	E	K	K	L	A	E	E	O	P
E	O	E	B	L	P	O	P	M	W	S	E	K	B	T	L	T	R
E	A	N	W	E	A	H	H	L	W	R	W	B	P	T	D	L	M
I	Y	N	N	P	M	H	G	R	A	H	H	A	M	O	N	T	L
N	F	I	E	Y	K	I	W	T	H	W	A	E	U	P	H	O	E
N	T	P	L	D	A	I	N	Y	A	E	L	L	H	S	A	R	P
W	E	S	H	H	C	R	N	M	A	E	E	M	E	U	O	N	P
L	S	L	E	E	E	E	D	P	I	R	A	H	R	W	E	T	L
K	O	L	I	N	O	I	G	H	S	E	G	I	L	W	L	D	H

HUMPBACK WHALE

SPOTTED DOLPHIN

Answers

FIN WHALE

SPINNER DOLPHIN

GRAY WHALE

Name Scramble

Unscramble the letters to form the names of these marine mammals.

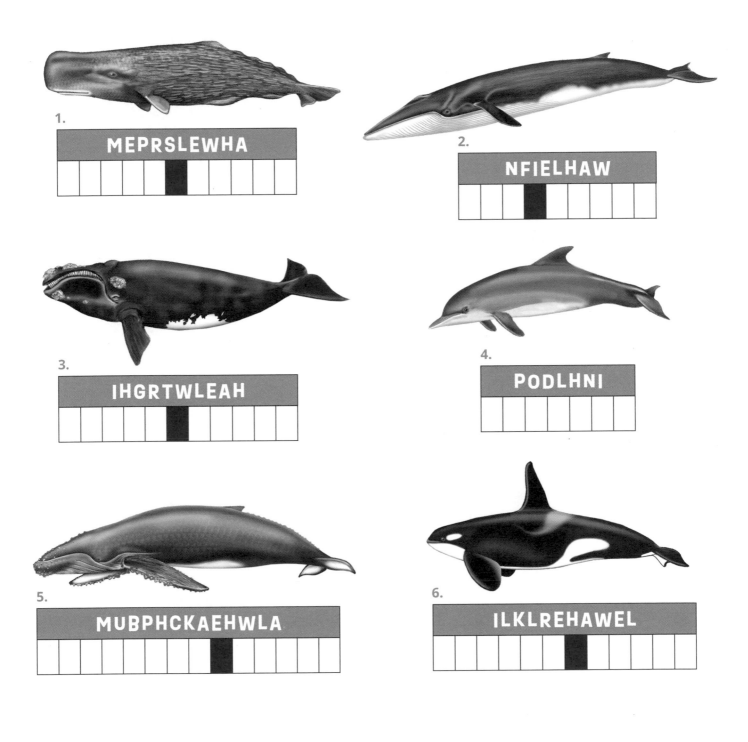

1.

MEPRSLEWHA

2.

NFIELHAW

3.

IHGRTWLEAH

4.

PODLHNI

5.

MUBPHCKAEHWLA

6.

ILKLREHAWEL

Word Search

Fishes are cold-blooded vertebrates that live in water and breathe oxygen that dissolved in the water through organs called gills. Most live in either saltwater or freshwater, though a few species divide their lives between the two. Fishes of the Texas seashore live in different habitats, including estuaries and shallow waters, open waters and reefs.

Find the names of these fishes of the Gulf of Mexico.

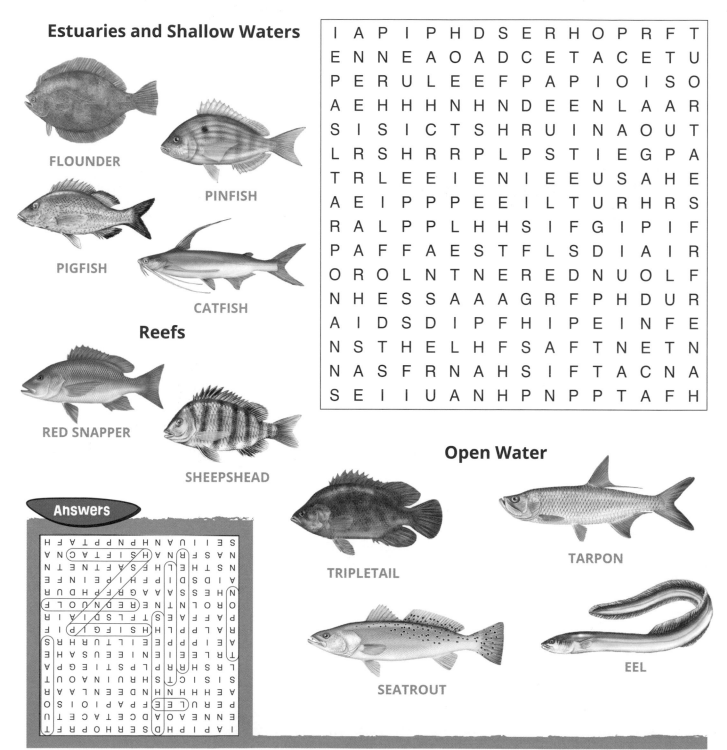

Estuaries and Shallow Waters

FLOUNDER

PINFISH

PIGFISH

CATFISH

Reefs

RED SNAPPER

SHEEPSHEAD

Answers

Open Water

TRIPLETAIL

TARPON

SEATROUT

EEL

Make Words

Common in tropical waters, there are at least 114 species of **Butterflyfish**. A close cousin of the angelfish, most are brightly colored in shades of yellow, white, black, blue, red and orange. Some have eyespots on their back ends, which helps confuse predators. Butterflyfish spend their time pecking their long snouts into coral and rock formations to hunt for coral polyps, worms and other small invertebrates.

How many words can you make from the letters in Butterflyfish?

_____   _____

_____   _____

_____   _____

_____   _____

_____   _____

_____   _____

_____   _____

_____   _____

Answers

Possible answers include: bit, bite, brute, buff, built, but, butter, buy, fife, fifty, filter, fish, fist, first, fit, flitter, flu, flub, flute, flutter, fly, fresh, fry, her, hilt, his, huff, lube, lye, rife, rub, rule, rye, shy, sift, silt, sir, sit, site, silt, slither, strife, strut, this, tier, tiff, tire, tribe, tries, trite, try, tub, yes

15

Name Scramble

Unscramble the letters to form the names of these familiar fishes.

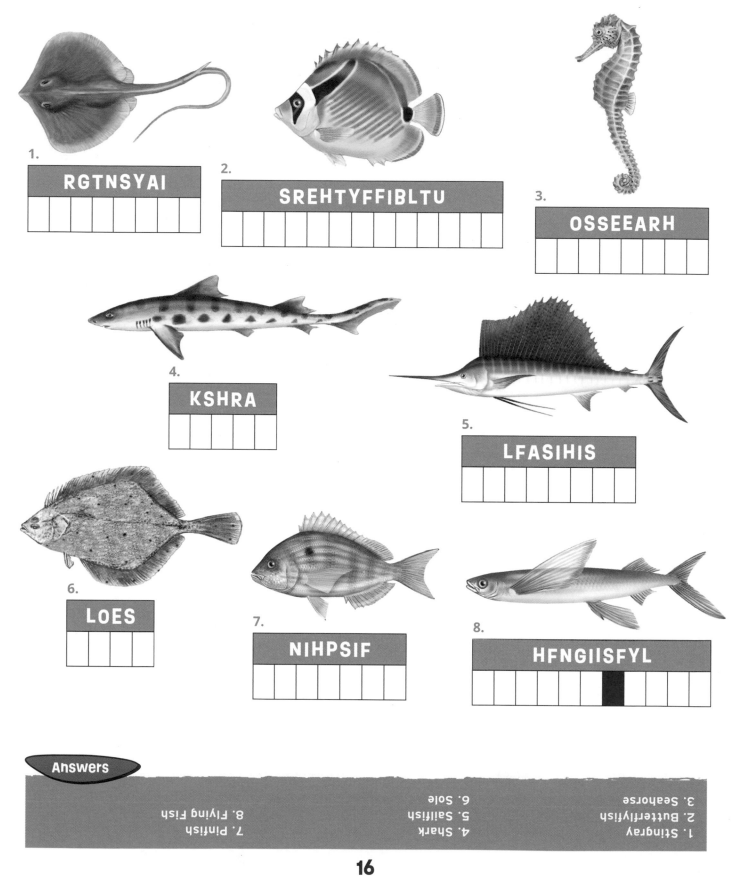

1. **RGTNSYAI**

2. **SREHTYFFIBLTU**

3. **OSSEEARH**

4. **KSHRA**

5. **LFASIHIS**

6. **LOES**

7. **NIHPSIF**

8. **HFNGIISFYL**

Origami

The **Atlantic Stingray** is a flat fish that feeds on worms, crabs, shellfish, shrimp and small fish at the bottom of the Gulf. It has a sharp barb at the base of its tail that can inject poison, but it will not attack unless it feels threatened. To avoid startling a stingray and being stung, shuffle your feet while walking into the surf or shallow waters. This is called the "stingray shuffle."

Starting with a square piece of paper, follow the simple folding instructions below to create a stingray.

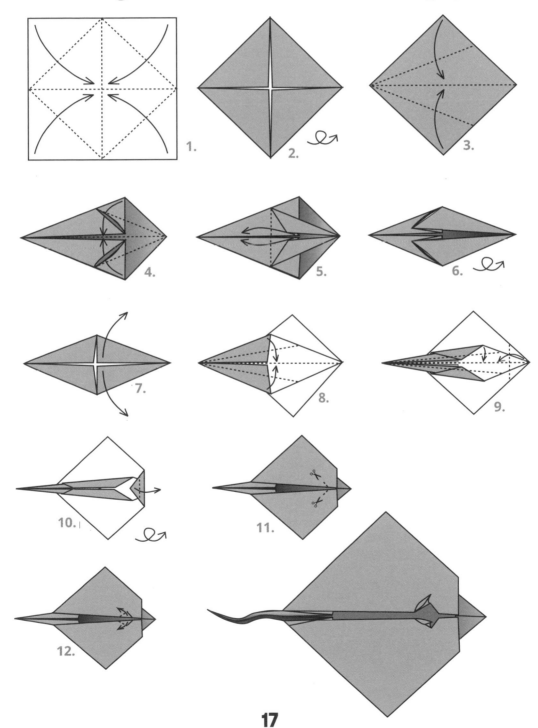

Maze

The **Great Barracuda** is a large predatory, ray-finned fish with a long mouth, sharp teeth and very powerful jaws. It is well-built for the hunt. Its silver sides and white belly make it hard to see among reefs in the open Gulf. Due to its large size, the barracuda has very few predators besides dolphins, sharks and Goliath groupers. This fish is an expert hunter but cannot eat a human—though it may charge toward you if you have any shiny objects with you in the water.

Help the Great Barracuda find its way to the anchovies as quickly as possible!

ENTER

Shadow Know-How

Now that you have learned several different species of saltwater fishes that live in the Gulf of Mexico, can you identify these?

1.

2. ☐☐☐

3. ☐☐☐☐☐ / ☐☐☐☐

☐☐☐☐☐☐☐☐

4. ☐☐☐☐☐☐☐☐☐

5. ☐☐☐☐☐

6. ☐☐☐☐☐☐☐☐☐☐ / ☐☐☐☐

7. ☐☐☐☐☐☐☐

8. ☐☐☐☐☐☐☐☐☐

Name Scramble

Reptiles are called "cold-blooded" and rely on the temperature of their environment to regulate their internal temperature. The most common types of reptiles in Texas are turtles, lizards, snakes and alligators. Amphibians are smooth-skinned animals that live in moist habitats and breathe through lungs, skin, gills or use all three. The most common amphibians in Texas are salamanders, frogs and toads.

Unscramble the names of these familiar reptiles and amphibians.

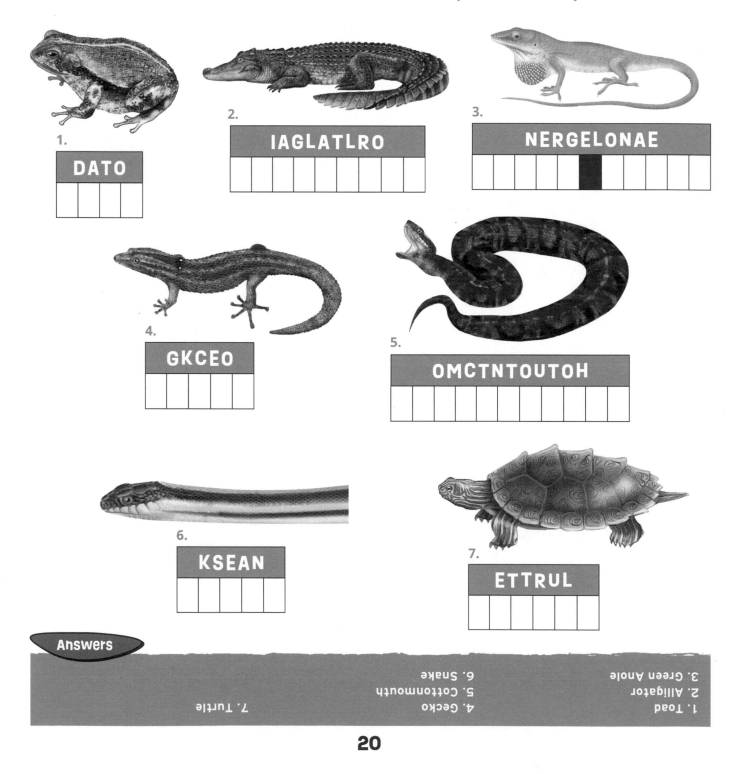

1. **DATO**

2. **IAGLATLRO**

3. **NERGELONAE**

4. **GKCEO**

5. **OMCTNTOUTOH**

6. **KSEAN**

7. **ETTRUL**

Name Match

Five species of sea turtle live off the coast of Texas. Sea turtles live most of their lives completely under water. They do breathe air but can remain underwater for hours. All species of sea turtle in the gulf are endangered, except for the loggerhead, and the loggerhead is classified as threatened. Endangered animals are in danger of becoming extinct. Threatened animals may soon become endangered if nothing is done to help them. Sea turtles only return to land to lay eggs, and most males never return.

Draw a line between the sea turtle and its name.

1.

A. KEMP'S RIDLEY SEA TURTLE

B. HAWKSBILL SEA TURTLE

4.

2.

C. LOGGERHEAD SEA TURTLE

3.

D. LEATHERBACK SEA TURTLE

5.

E. GREEN SEA TURTLE

1. This is the smallest and most endangered sea turtle.
2. This turtle is not named for the color of its shell but for the greenish color of its skin.
3. The most tropical species of sea turtle, it likes to stay near reefs to feed.
4. This is the largest and fastest-growing of all sea turtles. It can grow up to eight feet long and weigh 1300 pounds.
5. This sea turtle is a carnivore with powerful jaws. It feeds mostly on shellfish that live on the bottom of the ocean.

Answers

1: A, 2: E, 3: B, 4: D, 5: C

Origami

Starting with a square piece of paper, follow the simple folding instructions below to create a sea turtle.

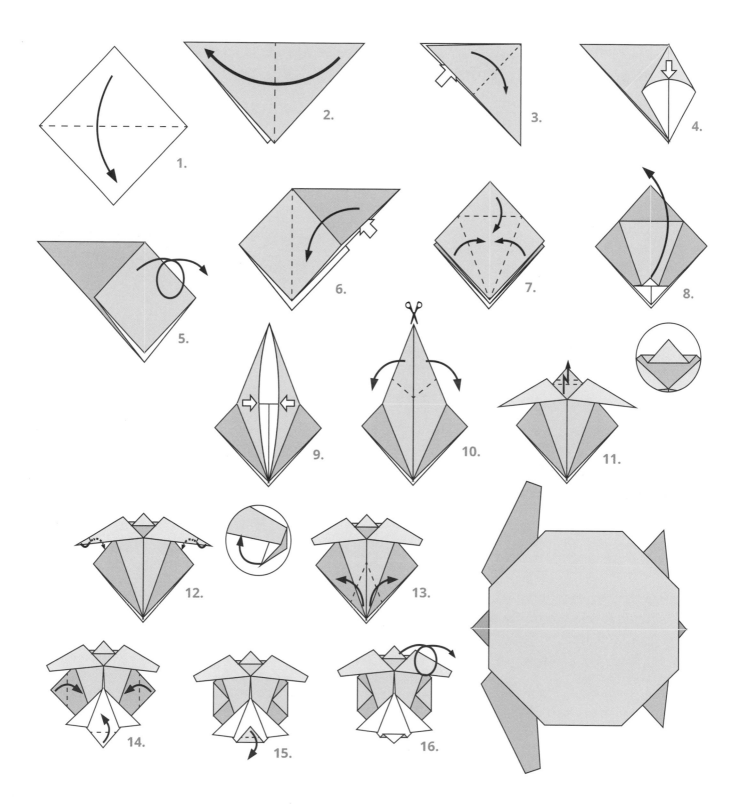

Be An Artist

Copy this Loggerhead Sea Turtle by drawing it one square at a time.

The **Loggerhead Sea Turtle** is the largest of all hard-shelled turtles. It has a large head with strong jaws. Its flippers work like wings in the water to help it stabilize and steer. It is a "keystone" species, which means that other animals in its ecosystem also depend on it for survival. An ecosystem is a community of living organisms that interact with each other and their environment.

Make Words

The **Alligator** is a large reptile that has tough skin and huge toothy jaws. Though it is related to crocodiles, you can tell it apart by its wide U-shaped snout. The alligator is a very good swimmer and often floats or swims with only its eyes and nostrils above water. A carnivore, the alligator will eat anything it can catch, including turtles, lizards, waterbirds, small mammals, snakes and even other alligators.

How many words can you make from the letters in its name?

_____   _____

_____   _____

_____   _____

_____   _____

_____   _____

_____   _____

_____   _____

_____   _____

_____   _____

24

Word Search

These sea creatures have something in common—they are all invertebrates, which means they do not have bones. These animals are an important part of the food web. Not only do they serve as food for birds, fish and mammals, but they also help break down organic matter in the ocean. Most need oxygen to live. Some have small gills. Others have little holes that absorb oxygen that has dissolved in the water. Some use breathing tubes that rise about the water's surface, and others bring air bubbles from the surface down under the water with them.

Find the names of the animals in this puzzle.

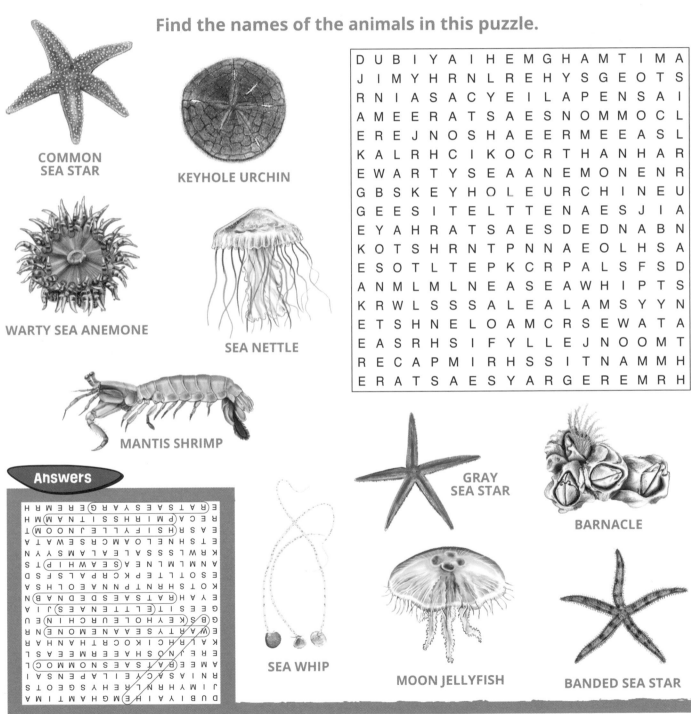

COMMON
SEA STAR

KEYHOLE URCHIN

WARTY SEA ANEMONE

SEA NETTLE

MANTIS SHRIMP

Answers

SEA WHIP

GRAY
SEA STAR

BARNACLE

MOON JELLYFISH

BANDED SEA STAR

Be An Artist

Draw this hermit crab by copying one square at a time.

The **Hermit Crab** is a small crab that protects itself by living in the shells of sea snails. It is often seen scurrying around on the sand and rocks near the water line. The shell acts like a mobile home. When threatened, it will withdraw all but its hard, protective claws into the shell.

Name Match

Draw a line between the animal and its name.

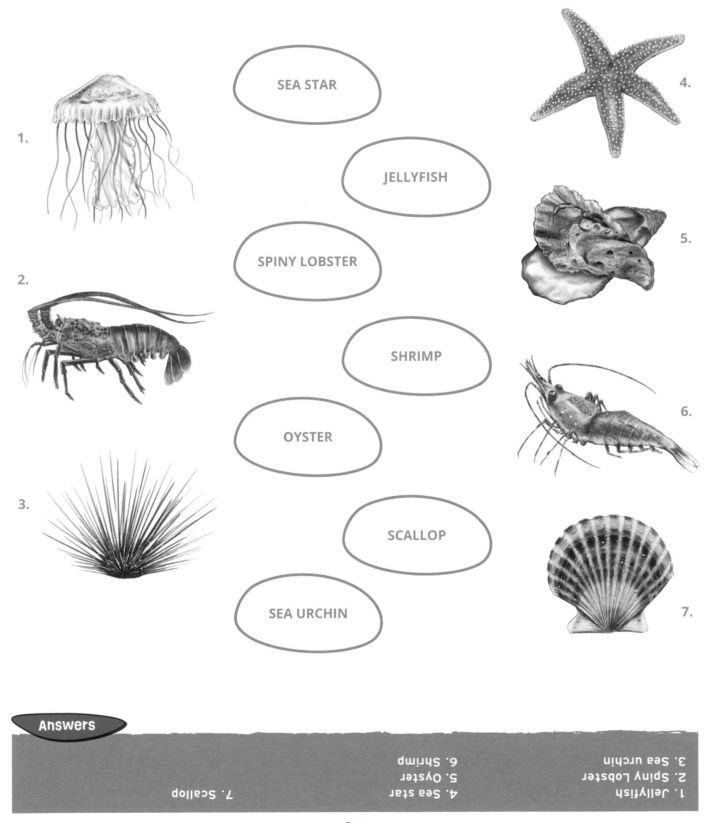

SEA STAR

JELLYFISH

SPINY LOBSTER

SHRIMP

OYSTER

SCALLOP

SEA URCHIN

1.

2.

3.

4.

5.

6.

7.

Word Search

A seashell is a protective exoskeleton formed by invertebrate animals that live in the sea. They are often found washed up on beaches. Animals that commonly produce seashells are mollusks, crabs, sea urchins, barnacles, brachiopods and annelid worms. Most seashells are external (on the outside), but some species form internal shells. Galveston Island off the Gulf Coast of Texas is one of the top places in the world for finding seashells.

Find the names of these unusual seashells in this puzzle.

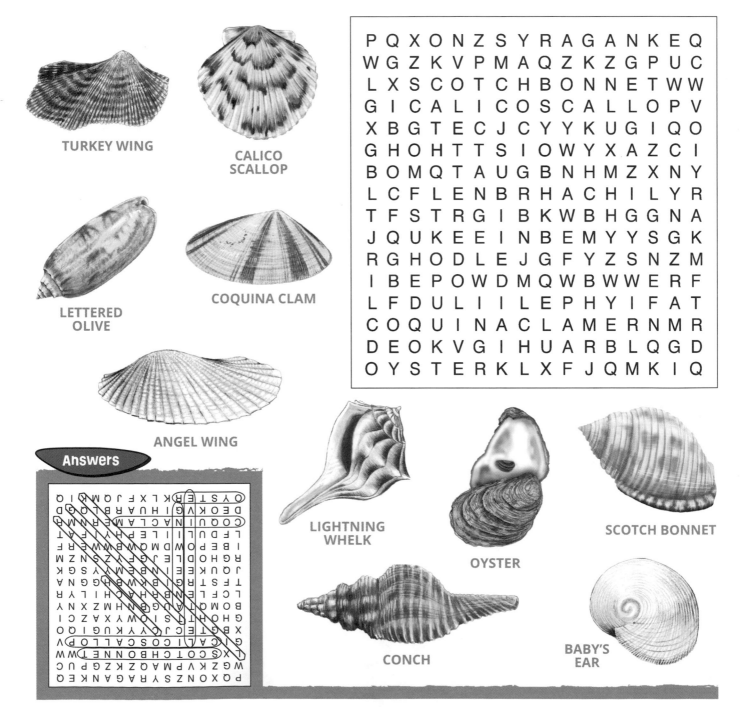

TURKEY WING

CALICO SCALLOP

```
P Q X O N Z S Y R A G A N K E Q
W G Z K V P M A Q Z K Z G P U C
L X S C O T C H B O N N E T W W
G I C A L I C O S C A L L O P V
X B G T E C J C Y Y K U G I Q O
G H O H T T S I O W Y X A Z C I
B O M Q T A U G B N H M Z X N Y
L C F L E N B R H A C H I L Y R
T F S T R G I B K W B H G G N A
J Q U K E E I N B E M Y Y S G K
R G H O D L E J G F Y Z S N Z M
I B E P O W D M Q W B W W E R F
L F D U L I I L E P H Y I F A T
C O Q U I N A C L A M E R N M R
D E O K V G I H U A R B L Q G D
O Y S T E R K L X F J Q M K I Q
```

LETTERED OLIVE

COQUINA CLAM

ANGEL WING

Answers

LIGHTNING WHELK

OYSTER

SCOTCH BONNET

CONCH

BABY'S EAR

Connect the Dots

Crustaceans live in freshwater and saltwater. They have hard external skeletons that support and protect their bodies. Shrimps, crabs, lobsters and crayfish are all common crustaceans.

Connect the dots to reveal this familiar Texas seashore crustacean.

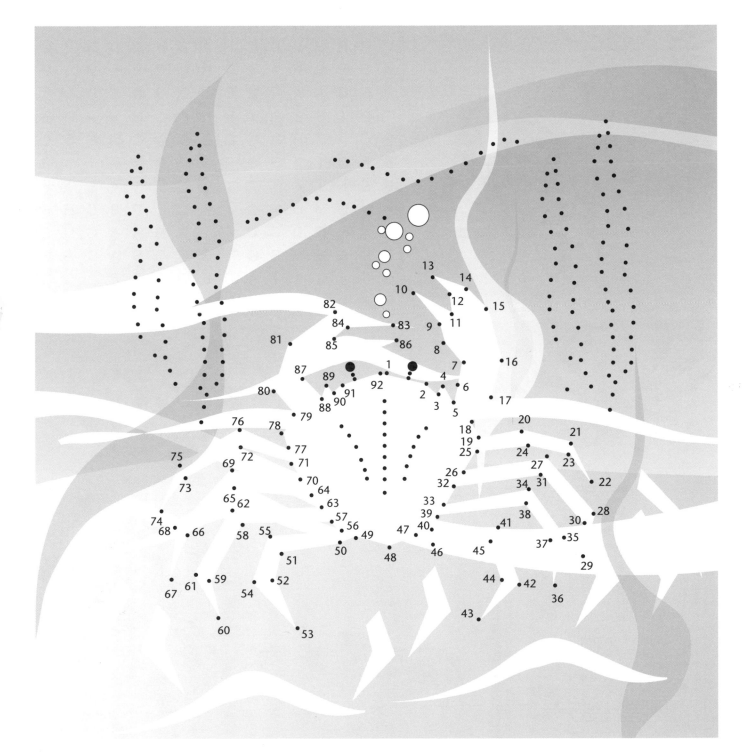

Word Search

Find the names of these common Gulf of Mexico crabs.

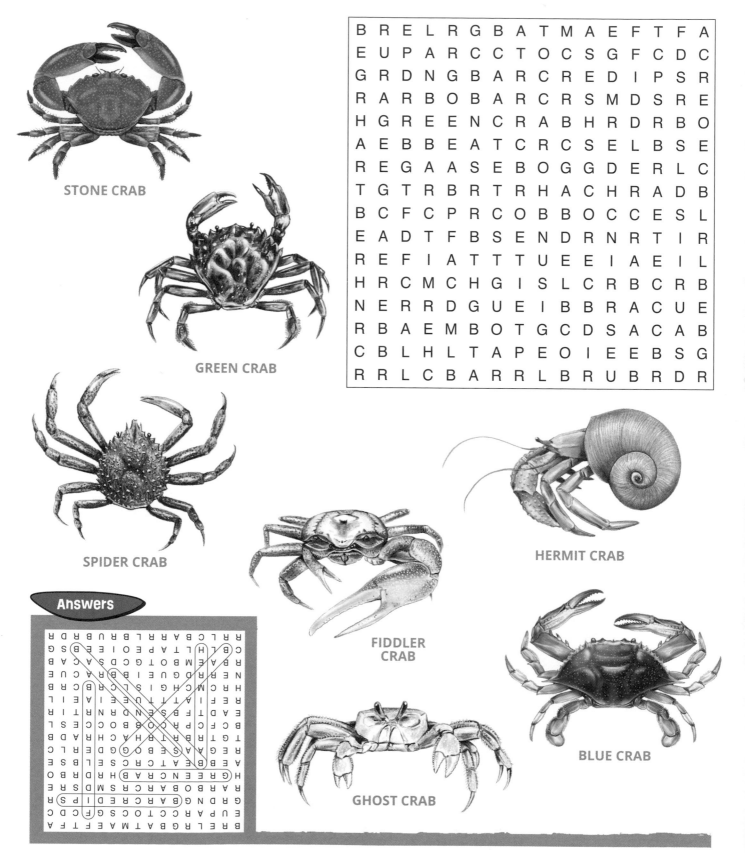

B R E L R G B A T M A E F T F A
E U P A R C C T O C S G F C D C
G R D N G B A R C R E D I P S R
R A R B O B A R C R S M D S R E
H G R E E N C R A B H R D R B O
A E B B E A T C R C S E L B S E
R E G A A S E B O G G D E R L C
T G T R B R T R H A C H R A D B
B C F C P R C O B B O C C E S L
E A D T F B S E N D R N R T I R
R E F I A T T U E E I A E I L
H R C M C H G I S L C R B C R B
N E R R D G U E I B B R A C U E
R B A E M B O T G C D S A C A B
C B L H L T A P E O I E E B S G
R R L C B A R R L B R U B R D R

STONE CRAB

GREEN CRAB

SPIDER CRAB

Answers

FIDDLER CRAB

HERMIT CRAB

BLUE CRAB

GHOST CRAB

Origami

The most common sea stars encountered in Gulf Coast waters are the Gray Sea Star, the Banded Sea Star and the Two-Spined Sea Star. They all lack suckers on the bottoms of their tube feet, which means they must swallow food whole and then regurgitate (bring back up) the parts they can't digest. Sea stars are known for their uncommon ability to grow new limbs as needed.

Starting with a square piece of paper, follow the simple folding instructions below to create a sea star.

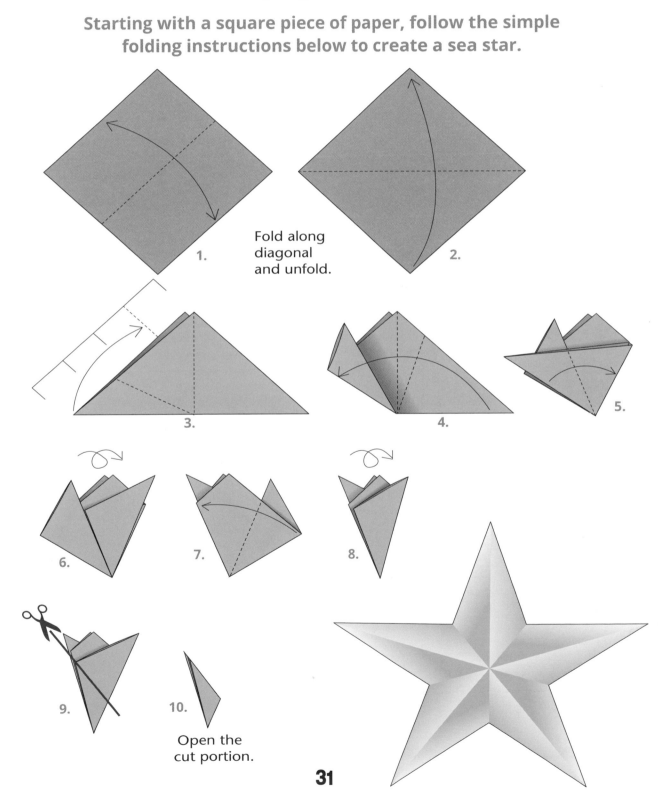

1.

Fold along diagonal and unfold.

2.

3.

4.

5.

6.

7.

8.

9.

10.

Open the cut portion.

31

Word Search

Because the Texas coast is constantly exposed to sea, wind and rain, the plants that grow near the Gulf of Mexico are known for their high salt tolerance. The coastal prairie along the Texas seashore is home to over 400 species of flowering plants. Vibrant wildflowers bloom every month of the year.

Find the names of these seashore plants in the puzzle.

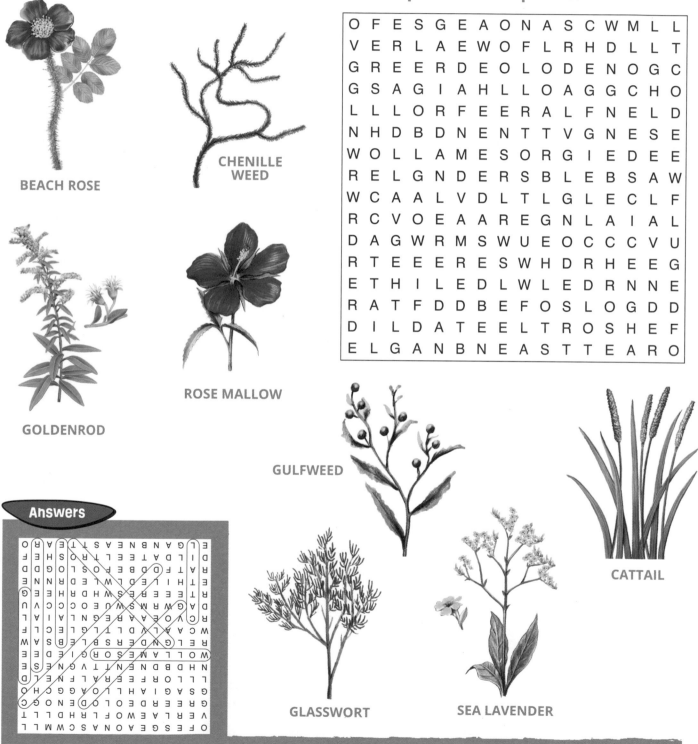

BEACH ROSE

CHENILLE WEED

```
O F E S G E A O N A S C W M L L
V E R L A E W O F L R H D L L T
G R E E R D E O L O D E N O G C
G S A G I A H L L O A G G C H O
L L L O R F E E R A L F N E L D
N H D B D N E N T T V G N E S E
W O L L A M E S O R G I E D E E
R E L G N D E R S B L E B S A W
W C A A L V D L T L G L E C L F
R C V O E A A R E G N L A I A L
D A G W R M S W U E O C C C V U
R T E E E R E S W H D R H E E G
E T H I L E D L W L E D R N N E
R A T F D D B E F O S L O G D D
D I L D A T E E L T R O S H E F
E L G A N B N E A S T T E A R O
```

GOLDENROD

ROSE MALLOW

GULFWEED

CATTAIL

Answers

```
E L G A N B N E A S T T E A R O
D I L D A T E E L T R O S H E F
R A T F D D B E F O S L O G D D
E T H I L E D L W L E D R N N E
R T E E E R E S W H D R H E E G
D A G W R M S W U E O C C C V U
R C V O E A A R E G N L A I A L
W C A A L V D L T L G L E C L F
R E L G N D E R S B L E B S A W
W O L L A M E S O R G I E D E E
N H D B D N E N T T V G N E S E
L L L O R F E E R A L F N E L D
G S A G I A H L L O A G G C H O
G R E E R D E O L O D E N O G C
V E R L A E W O F L R H D L L T
O F E S G E A O N A S C W M L L
```

GLASSWORT

SEA LAVENDER